What Do We Have to Get?

Written by Kelly T. Gabrysch

Illustrated by Mark Hicks

Mom said, "Get ten yams,
a can of ham,
and red jam."

Jan and Ed went to the store.

They went to get ten yams,
a can of ham,
and red jam.

They met Nan.

They met Dan.

They met Ted and stopped to pet his cat.

They got to the store.

"What do we have to get?" asked Jan.

"What do we have to get?" asked Ed.

"Ten hams," said Jan.

"Are you sure?"

"Yes."

11

"A can of pop," said Ed.

"Are you sure?"

"Yes."

"And red candy," said Jan and Ed.

Mom saw the ten hams,
the can of pop,
and the red candy.

Jan and Ed went back to the store ...

with a list.